GET YOUR SHIFT TOGETHER:

What Did Goldilocks Know about Building and Maintaining Resilience?

Keith Kesler, DO   Sarah Brisiel, BA

"I am not afraid of storms for I am learning how to sail my ship." - Louisa May Alcott

WELCOME

We launched Clinician2Coach, a coaching and consulting business to help people bring their best and most creative self to every engagement, both personally and professionally. Since then, we have spent time speaking, leading communication clinics and development workshops, and investing in transformational work. Often after a speaking engagement, we are asked if we have any supplemental materials, or additional information about the subjects we invite people to think about. This book is our response. We use this in conjunction with in-person seminars and workshops to provide the most complete experience possible for our clients and participants. We hope it acts as a useful tool to forward personal and professional growth.

Here's to your continued success!

-Keith and Sarah

CONTENTS

A Note to Readers

Everyone wants the Holy Grail of
Solution Sets.
But unless we help you understand how to
cultivate the muscle of resilience, we'd just be
handing out another list from the self help
section.

This is the handbook to help exercise that
muscle.

Goldilocks.

Let's Use The Children's Tale As A Framework For Understanding Resilience.

What's the story?

The story of Goldilocks has evolved through the ages.

For the purpose of this discussion, the essential story boils down to this:

- Young girl gets lost in the woods.
- She finds a house owned by Three Bears.
- She breaks into the house- hungry, tired, and scared.
- She finds three bowls of porridge on the table and helps herself.
- The first bowl of porridge is too hot.
- The second bowl of porridge is too cold.
- The third bowl of porridge is 'just right', and she eats it all.

By using Goldilocks, you now have a target to shoot for in the discussion of resilience... You are shooting for **'just right**.'

Shift.

The Constant Oscillation Between States Of Stress And Recovery. The Constant Reality of Being Alive. When Shift Stops-You Die!

What is stress?

One definition of stress is simply stimulation. Stress is your body's way of responding to any kind of demand.

Normal stress

Normal stress is not only a natural part of life, but can motivate you, create change, and provide excitement. Stress is an inescapable part of the human condition. Normal stress is anything that affects your actions, emotions, decisions, or desires. Anything that stimulates you is technically a stressor.

Exceptional stress

Stress gets bad press. You are told to decrease stress and avoid stress by the media, by your doctors, and by your peers. But what they are talking about is exceptional stress. It is chronic, consistent, unremitting stress, and leads to illness, fatigue, and a veritable laundry list of health and wellness challenges.

What is recovery?

Recovery is the necessary time and effort it takes for you to acclimate and adjust to new stimuli. Webster defines recovery as a return to a normal state of health, mind, or strength. In this work rest is synonymous with recovery.

Normal recovery

Normal rest is essential for both growth and development. Allowing time for recovery provides the opportunity for reinforcing the learned behavior, trait, skill, or muscle being developed. Growth, change, and development begun in times of stress take root and grow during times of recovery.

Exceptional recovery

Like exceptional stress, prolonged exceptional rest must be avoided. Too much time spent in recovery creates stagnation, apathy, atrophy, and disengagement.

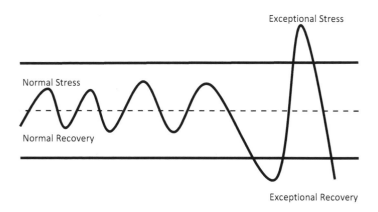

Exceptional Stress

Normal Stress

Normal Recovery

Exceptional Recovery

Resilience

When someone describes resilience as the ability to bounce back from the inevitable challenges of life, it creates confusion. That definition has no appreciable measuring stick or map, therefore it is confusing to know what next right action is necessary to cultivate a sense of resilience.

Being **'Between the Lines'** of normal stress and normal recovery is what defines resilience. YOU CAN LEARN AND DEVELOP RESILIENCE. It is not a genetic gift or predetermined state.

Staying within that resilient sweet spot can be challenging. But like muscles, you can hone, strengthen, and improve your ability to:
1. Stay in that sweet spot.
2. Recognize when you have slipped out of it.

How can you tell when you have arrived?

Do you want to consistently and sustainably bring your best self to the table? Then examine the moments when you know you're outside the lines of resilience. Remember Goldilocks? The first bowl of porridge was too hot, the second was too cold, but the third was JUST RIGHT. Apply the Goldilocks Method. Too much stress? Too much rest? We are shooting for 'just right'... The sweet spot of resilience. (SEE APPENDIX K)

Why should you bother?

"Resilience is a REFLEX, a way of facing and understanding the world that is deeply etched into a person's mind and soul.
Resilient people and companies face reality with staunchness, make meaning of hardship instead of crying out in despair, and improvise solutions from thin air." Diane L Coutu, Harvard Business Review

It really is just that simple.

The Four Quadrants Of Resilience.

There are four distinct quadrants of resilience: Physical, Spiritual, Mental, and Emotional. In order to build effective, sustainable resilience all four need to be in balance.

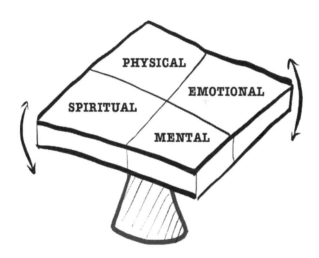

Imagine four quadrants on a single plane. The plane is balanced on a fulcrum in constant oscillation and movement.

Overview

Remembering that resilience is living 'Between the Lines', look at the relative balance of each quadrant balanced on that fulcrum. Oscillation, or shift, is now occurring up-and-down, side to side, and spinning on that fulcrum.

Looking at each quadrant in isolation is a useful exercise to gain clarity about your own resilience, but remember that all four of these quadrants are essentially integrated. There is a constant interplay and overlap between all four quadrants.

"More than education, more than experience, more than training, a person's level of resilience will determine who succeeds and who fails. That's true in the cancer ward, it's true in the Olympics, and it's true in the boardroom." Dean Becker, CEO Adaptiv Learning Systems

Physical

This is the most straightforward area of focus. The Physical Quadrant is simply your corpus: the bone, skin, muscles, sensory organs and the brain. It is the instrument you use to gain information and navigate about the world around you. The Physical Quadrant is the vehicle for your **actions**.

Spiritual

For the purposes of this model, the Spiritual Quadrant is the source of the **values** that define, drive, and determine your actions. It is the source of meaning, purpose, and connection.

Mental

Cognitive and intellectual thought are the basis of the Mental Quadrant. This quadrant is most readily accessed in your profession or career, and is the quadrant most responsible for making rational and logical **decisions**.

Emotional

Emotional Intelligence is the most important part of this quadrant (in terms of Resilience). This is not simply the feeling states associated with emotion. Instead focus on how you make emotions work for you instead of against you. The Emotional Quadrant is the source for your **reactions** to situations and circumstances.

The Three Bears.

Goldilocks provides a helpful method for evaluating whether or not you are staying 'Between the Lines'. The Three Bears offer a way to understand what goes on within your brain to keep you 'Between the Lines' (or not).

The Three Bears or The Tripartite Brain

Obviously there is only one brain in your head, but you use three distinct parts of your brain when you make decisions, react to situations, assign value to your circumstances, or take actions.

Baby Bear- (Gut). This is the most primitive and primal part of the brain. Sometimes known as lizard brain, this system is reflexive, automatic, subconscious, and associated with the flight/fright response. Anatomically, this system is run by the brainstem, the amygdala, and the thalamus. Think about babies. They are ruled entirely by their instinct. Hungry! Tired! Scared! Cold! Baby Bear brain is entirely focused on survival. Baby Bear most directly engages the world at the level of instinct and intuition.

Mama Bear- (Heart). Also known as the mammalian brain, Mama Bear is like many mamas- nostalgic and emotional. Mama Bear is activated in relationships and social connections. The limbic system, (one of Mama Bear's other identifiers), is the center of memory of past experience. Mama Bear tracks patterns of experience and assigns an emotional attachment to these patterns. She attaches value and emotion to circumstances and relationships. Mama Bear is the most involved in reaching out and connecting to the world.

Papa Bear- (Head). Papa Bear is like a 1950s stereotype of the male patriarch. Unemotional, distant, logical, and data-driven, Papa Bear is the most recently evolved part of our brain. Located in the Neo-cortex, Prefrontal Cortex, and Frontal Cortex, this part of the brain is the most rational, conscious, reflective, and highly cognitive part of the brain. Papa Bear provides reason and adherence to cultural norms. Papa Bear is the most engaged in observation of the world and the creation of detailed future plans.

For true **'Between the Lines'** resilience, two things must happen:
1. You must acknowledge that all Three Bears exist, play essential roles, and are equally valuable.
2. You must pay close attention and dedicate time, energy, and effort into keeping all Three Bears in alignment.

Remember, looking at each Quadrant of Resilience in isolation is only an instructional exercise designed to help give you a method for self-evaluation and self-awareness. Just like the Quadrants, The Three Bears never operate in isolation. The Four Quadrants and the Three Bears are always involved in a simultaneous and integrated dance. Maintaining equilibrium and balance within the Four Quadrants and amongst the Three Bears is essential to maintaining resilience.

BABY BEAR	MAMA BEAR	PAPA BEAR
GUT	HEART	HEAD
LIZARD BRAIN	MAMMALIAN BRAIN	HUMAN BRAIN
UNCONSCIOUS	SUBCONSCIOUS	CONSCIOUS
SAFE/NOT SAFE?	PAST EXPERIENCE	CULTURAL
FLIGHT/FRIGHT/FREEZE	MODIFIES ACTIONS	PROVIDES LOGIC & REASON
FULL TILT BOOGIE!!	CONNECTS WITH OTHERS	OBSERVES THE WORLD
IMMEDIATE/DIRECT	IMAGES/DREAMS/MEMORIES	DETAILED FUTURE PLANS

Physical.

Taking care of the Physical Quadrant is the foundation for resilient fitness in all quadrants.

Actions

The Physical Quadrant is the vehicle for your **actions**. It is the easiest quadrant in which to understand the oscillation between optimal stress and optimal recovery. Weight training programs use stress and recovery to build and develop muscles. True strength and growth happen only when stress occurs and is followed by recovery.

"Physical fitness is defined as the ability to carry out daily tasks with vigor and alertness, without undue fatigue, and with ample energy to enjoy leisure time pursuits and respond to emergencies."
US Center for Disease Control

Goldilocks In The Physical Quadrant

The Goldilocks Method for Understanding Resilience			
	Too Much Stress/Stimulation	"Just Right" Resilience Sweet Spot	Not Enough Too Much Recovery
		CDC- ability to carry out	
	Injury	daily taskes with vigor	Atrophy
Physical	Impairment	and alertness, no undue	Weakness
	Pain	fatigue, with ample energy	Exhaustion
	Overuse	to enjoy leisure and	Disease
		respond to emergency	

The Bears and the Physical Quadrant

All three parts of the brain need to be in alignment for Physical Resilience. In this quadrant, Baby Bear gets things started- (eating, sleeping, and exercise are essential for survival). However, if you rely exclusively on Baby Bear to maintain your Physical Resilience, you're fighting a losing battle. Baby Bear gets its needs met with potato chips and soda just as easily as with leafy greens and lean proteins.

Papa Bear must get involved for determining and tracking the metrics necessary for change. (What is your blood pressure? Do you need lab work? Are you eating the correct calories for your activity level? Are you sleeping deeply and for long enough each night?) Without the data-driven influence of Papa Bear, there is no accurate way to gauge success, or track change.

And don't forget Mama Bear. Mama Bear is responsible for the dopamine hit and limbic system engagement that encourages and rewards the kinds of behavior designed to strengthen Physical Resilience. You know when you go to the gym and feel great after? That is Mama Bear in her element.

Factors That Influence Physical Resilience

Inflammation

Inflammation has a profound effect on the body and mind. The body's immune response to threats is a throwback to our predecessors' need to find physical safety and survive exposure to disease. Long-term, systemic inflammation acts as a hurdle to creating sustainable resilience. Inflammation is the primary mechanism for chronic illness including arthritis, diabetes, and heart disease. Without first ruling out inflammatory causes of malaise, impulsivity, and reactionary behavior, working to build resilience can feel a bit like banging your head against a brick wall. (SEE APPENDIX E)

Self-Care

Diet, Exercise, and Sleep all play a integral part in your health and resiliency. None of this is new information. You have been exposed to this information and yet you do not act on it. (Very few people do!) There is never 'enough time', you promise yourself that you'll 'do it tomorrow', or just simply do not prioritize it. You discount the benefit to yourself. (This phenomenon is called temporal discounting.) There are hundreds of studies that show the benefit of self-care. The trick is to **create systems** to help you adhere to those pesky resolutions you make over and over and over and over again.

Question: What prevents you from taking care of yourself?

Actionable steps:

- 6 To 8 Hours of Sleep Each Night
- Physical Exercise and Activity 3 to 4 Times a Week
- Regular Adherence to Healthy Nutrition
- Food Journal
- Sleep Journal
- Seinfeld Tracking Sheet (GOLD STARS!)

Spiritual.

The Spiritual Quadrant provides the driving force for your life. It is how you define what is valuable to you, and how you determine where to spend your time and energy.

Values

The Spiritual Quadrant is based on your unique **values** system. A value is a guide for behavior. Values allow you to determine what is good, beautiful, useful, worth having, and worth striving for. This is not necessarily about getting to a Mosque, Temple, Synagogue, or Church. (Although for some, it is central and essential to their Spiritual Resilience.) Rather, it is a sense that there is something bigger than yourself- and being a part of it. That sense of meaning and purpose combined with acting in alignment with your Values is essential for Spiritual Resilience.

"Spiritual fitness is the development of positive and helpful beliefs, practices, and connecting expressions of the human spirit." U.S. Army's Soldier And Family Fitness Program

Goldilocks In The Spiritual Quadrant

The Goldilocks Method for Understanding Resilience			
	Too Much Stress/Stimulation	"Just Right" Resilience Sweet Spot	Not Enough Too Much Recovery
Spiritual	Hyper-Religiosiy	Clarity of Values	Loss of purpose
	Judgement	Sense of Connection	Existentially Lost
	Fundamentalism	Belonging to something	Loss of Meaning
	Legalism	bigger than oneself	Lethargy
		(Community, Family,God)	

The Bears And The Spiritual Quadrant

Spiritual resilience is attainable if all Three Bears are in alignment. The Spiritual Quadrant is Mama Bear's domain. She is the default leader here. The limbic system (where Mama Bear reigns supreme) is where memories are made, processed, and stored. Lived experiences profoundly affect your inherent value system. Both consciously and unconsciously, Mama Bear is guiding your determination of what feels right. Do you know why you're motivated by beauty? Can you explain it? Or does it simply feel right? Mama Bear needs no explanation other than that.

Baby Bear is about instinctive gratification, not meeting needs based on core values. When Baby Bear gets overinvolved, your value systems get ignored in order to accommodate survival. When Baby Bear is appropriately engaged, the values that matter to you are taken into account-even when satisfying the basic needs for Baby Bear.

Papa attempts to intellectualize values which can be off-putting and distancing to people. But when appropriately engaged and in alignment with Mama Bear, Papa Bear helps give you the language and the metrics to identify your value system and take your values into account when making decisions.

Factors that influence Spiritual Resilience

Exploration And Defining Your Values

Understanding what really matters to you is the first step in building Spiritual Resilience. Without specific and intentional work, you can absorb values that do not necessarily resonate with you. (SEE APPENDIX J)

Compelling Why

Your compelling why is your story, and how you got to be where you are. You are necessarily (even at times unwillingly) affected by the world, friends, family, and culture. Working backwards from your story you can trace the patterns that you see. Are you motivated by beauty? Altruism? Money? Power? Peace? When you examine the whys of your decision-making, it can help clarify your unique value system. (SEE APPENDIX I)

Gratitude

"Comparison is thief of joy." Theodore Roosevelt

Teddy had it right. In discussing resilience, gratitude can act as a barometer or warning to help identify when you're out of alignment with your values. At its core, your human tendency to compare and contrast yourself to others can undermine your inner peace. Essentially, it causes you to evaluate your 'insides based on someone else's outsides'.

When are you able to easily and readily access gratitude? When you have clarity about your personal values and alignment with those values in your daily life.

Mindfulness

Mindfulness is a practice and exercise of sustained focus and attention. When in practice, Mindfulness strengthens the capacity for moment to moment self-awareness.

To help you understand the value of mindfulness and strengthening spiritual fitness and resilience, think about the steps you'd take to recover from a knee injury. When the knee is involved, physical therapists will recommend strengthening the supportive and neighboring muscles to ultimately recover a full range of motion. Mindfulness is like a neighboring muscle to resilience. Practicing a stance of mindfulness strengthens the muscles of resilience. Navigating the shift of life so you can stay Between the Lines requires the attention and focus that is developed through mindfulness training. (SEE APPENDIX C)

Question: What are your unique values? Are you living in alignment with your values? (SEE APPENDIX J)

Actionable Steps:

- Gratitude Journal (SEE APPENDIX D)
- Meditation Practice (SEE APPENDIX C)
- Values Worksheet (SEE APPENDIX J)
- Compelling Why Worksheet (SEE APPENDIX I)
- Spiritual Reading And Counsel

Mental.

The ability to reason, learn, plan for the future, and adapt lies within the Mental Quadrant.

Decisions

The Mental Quadrant is the seat of your logical and rational decision-making. Like muscle growth in the Physical Quadrant, you can strengthen your Mental Resilience to become more strategic, impactful, and creative decision-makers. Trying to make a decision 'outside the lines' of resilience is like making decisions when drunk.

Goldilocks In The Mental Quadrant

The Goldilocks Method for Understanding Resilience			
	Too Much Stress/Stimulation	"Just Right" Resilience Sweet Spot	Not Enough Too Much Recovery
Mental	Errors in Judgment	Focus	Indecisive
	Rigidity	Creativity	Foggy thinking
	Inflexibility of thinking	Freshness	Low risk tolerance
	Impulsivity	Risk Tolerant	Avoidance
	Cognitive Closure	Clarity	

The Bears And The Mental Quadrant

All of the Three Bears need to be in alignment for optimal Mental Resilience and fitness. In this quadrant, Papa Bear is the default leader of the parade. Thinking, processing, future planning, and many of the cognitive functions needed in the workplace (and in our lives) are driven by Papa Bear.

Mama Bear is most often blamed for interfering with the rational clarity of Papa. In Western culture particularly, there's a myth that you only make good decisions when exercising cold, logical analysis. In reality, Mama Bear plays an essential role within the Mental Quadrant. Mama is primarily responsible for navigating emotional memories and the meaning associated with them. She is the seat of empathy. It is only when Mama Bear and Papa Bear are fully in alignment that you are capable of making creative, strategic decisions. In fact, functional MRIs have demonstrated that the strongest creative thinkers utilize both Mama Bear and Papa Bear equally in tandem. To depend entirely on Papa Bear guarantees rigid and inflexible thinking when under pressure.

Baby Bear is always at work within the Mental Quadrant. In every interaction from the boardroom to the mailroom, Baby Bear is assessing danger and making decisions about the situation and people you are interacting with. Safe/Unsafe? Like/Unlike? Friend/Foe? Baby Bear is primarily responsible for the intuitive gut instinct about hiring an assistant, or leaving a sale on the table.

Factors That Influence Mental Resilience

Behavioral Economics

We like to believe that we are creatures of cold logic, and able to look at any given problem with clarity and distance, but the truth is quite different. Humans are predictably irrational. This is so common that if you ignore this propensity in yourself it will keep you out of the 'just right' spot and consistently in a state a frustration. Your penchant for making illogical decisions is so common that it has birthed an entire field of study (behavioral economics). (SEE APPENDIX B)

Cognitive Blind Spots Or Biases

When one or more of the Bears gets *over*involved, you become prone to making errors in judgment. For example, when Mama Bear or Baby Bear get overinvolved or out of alignment with Papa Bear, logic dies. You become prone to making errors in thinking, processing information, and judgment. (SEE APPENDIX A)

Neurogenesis

You actually generate new brain tissue and create new neural pathways through new experiences. That process is called *neurogenesis*.

In terms of strengthening the cognitive muscles for Mental Resilience, this is exceptionally good news. By focusing on new and novel experiences you naturally expand your viewpoints, avoid rigidity in your thinking, and are able to access different and more creative problem-solving approaches.

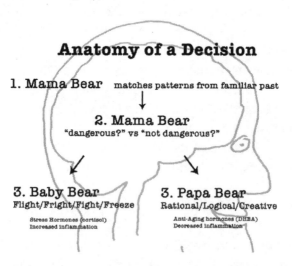

Anatomy of a Decision

1. Mama Bear   matches patterns from familiar past

↓

2. Mama Bear
"dangerous?" vs "not dangerous?"

3. Baby Bear
Flight/Fright/Fight/Freeze
Stress Hormones (cortisol)
Increased inflammation

3. Papa Bear
Rational/Logical/Creative
Anti-Aging hormones (DHEA)
Decreased inflammation

Question: Where are the places where you are stuck in your thinking and problem solving? Where do you get concrete and rigid in your thinking?

Actionable steps:

- Take a class (any class)
- Learn a new language
- Learn an instrument

- Book an adventure trip for novelty
- Expose yourself to as many new experiences as possible
- Play hard! Schedule time to be silly. (Humor is essential for cognitive fitness.)
- Challenge your existing mindset
- Adopt a protégé, someone to mentor

Emotional.

Emotional Intelligence is key to resilience within the Emotional Quadrant.

Reactions

The Emotional Quadrant is the seat of your **reactions** to situations and circumstances. To remain resilient within the Emotional Quadrant, it is essential that you understand the concept of Emotional Intelligence. Emotional Intelligence includes four major capacities: emotional self-awareness, emotional self-regulation, empathy, and social skills.

Emotional Self Awareness: The capacity to feel and identify your emotions and how they affect your decision-making.
Emotional Self-regulation: The necessary ability to control and redirect your emotional reactions to situations that arise both internally and externally.
Empathy: The capacity to understand the mood of those with whom you interact-both personally and professionally.
Social Skills: The capacity to establish and maintain social interactions and relationships (especially under stressful circumstances).

Goldilocks In The Emotional Quadrant

The Goldilocks Method for Understanding Resilience			
	Too Much Stress/Stimulation	"Just Right" Resilience Sweet Spot	Not Enough Too Much Recovery
Emotional	Frustration	Self aware	Depression
	Anxiety	Understand how emotions	Apathy
	Projection	affect other, and how	Withdrawal
	Anger	their emotions affect you	Social Isolation
	Irritability	Joyful	Confusion
		Content	

The Bears And The Emotional Quadrant

Again, alignment of the Three Bears is essential for Emotional Resilience. Mama Bear is the major player in this quadrant, but both Papa and Baby have their essential roles. Mama Bear feels the feelings and is affected by the feelings of others. Papa Bear assists Mama Bear by giving her words to describe the feelings, but that presents a slippery slope. You can sometimes avoid actually feeling the emotion by demonstrating a great vocabulary of feeling words. (This is referred to as *intellectualizing* by psychologists.) Remember the key to strong Emotional Resilience is understanding that you cannot think your way through the emotions.

And then there's Baby Bear. In terms of Emotional Resilience, Baby Bear's involvement is primarily reactive. When triggered by an external (or internal) stimuli, Baby Bear basically screams at you. Baby Bear is responsible for the flight, flight, freeze response to intense emotional stimuli.

When all Three Bears are working together, you are able to navigate emotional stimuli with a degree of equanimity. You can pause, take note of Baby Bear's reactive response, and then access the combined contribution of Mama and Papa Bear. When they are not in alignment, you're more likely to be impulsive, reactive, and illogical in your decisions and actions. In short, true Emotional Resilience is a fluid connection between Mama, Papa and Baby Bear.

Factors that influence Emotional Resilience

Shame

Shame sabotages success, and definitely sabotages resilience. You know shame. Your heart beats hard, your stomach clenches, you blush, and you avoid eye contact. It is the deeply rooted, painfully felt feeling of worthlessness. The challenge is to recognize shame for what it is and to cultivate an internal understanding that refuses to submit to shame and instead rewards your vulnerability. For more info, Brené Brown does excellent work on vulnerability. (SEE APPENDIX M)

Imposter Syndrome

Imposter Syndrome, an all too common belief that you are 'faking it' or being a 'poser', will profoundly affect your resilience. Unable to access the truth of your own success or power, your capacity to stay 'Between the Lines' of resilience will be negligible.

Imposter Syndrome can be broken down into a few key components:

- You are unable to recognize your own accomplishments.
- Dismiss success as luck, good timing, or deceit.
- Feel as if you have misrepresented yourself, or have been misrepresented.
- Think your bosses and superiors overestimate their ability, knowledge, or skill.

(SEE APPENDIX H)

Question: How are your emotions co-opting or enhancing your decision-making?

Actionable Steps:

- Active And Conscious Listening
- Crucial Conversations
- Relationship Evaluation
- EQi 2.0 profiling
- Coaching
- Meditation Practice

APPENDIX

APPENDIX A
COGNITIVE BLIND SPOTS

"Although we assume intelligence is a buffer against bias...it can actually be a subtle curse." *Jonah Lehrer- "Why Smart People are Stupid"*

Chances are you have heard the term Blind Spot or Cognitive Bias. Social and traditional media are full of discussions about Blind Spots and their effects. But if Lehrer is correct, you are most likely dismissing them as irrelevant. Articles aimed at avoiding your Blind Spots and their damaging effects "don't really apply to me." Or you smugly respond, "I can name three different Blind Spots of mine-clearly I can avoid them (and by the way, I am smarter than everyone else who can't!)"

In fact, the more educated you are, or the higher up the food chain you are professionally and personally, the more likely you are to be affected and misguided by your cognitive Blind Spots! **Translation: the smarter you are, the dumber your decisions can be!** The people who successfully navigate around their Blind Spots have an unfair competitive advantage over those who remain blind to them. (Pun intended).

Brain Matters

When we were cave-dwelling Neanderthals, our brains' primary function was to make instantaneous decisions to help keep us out of harm's way. Make the wrong decision and the dinosaur at the front of the cave ate you. The part of the brain responsible for this kind of thinking is the Amygdala (what I call the Lizard Brain or Baby Bear). Neanderthals gave their Amygdala a workout. Decision-making was exclusively automatic, instantaneous, unconscious, and motivated by the need to survive. Fast forward. Our modern-day Amygdala retains the same urges. Motivated to protect us from harm, it constantly scans our surroundings for dangers real and imagined! **But unfortunately our brains cannot differentiate between a dinosaur and a loaded conversation with our Director of Operations!** Our brain tells us we're going to get eaten and so we respond the same physically and psychically.

Let's look at what drives our modern day **Baby Bear/Lizard Brain:**

• **The Need to Feel Right/Certain-** It is essential for Baby Bear/Lizard Brain to feel right, to feel certain. Uncertainty creates huge amounts of anxiety for Baby Bear/Lizard Brain.
• **The Need to Feel in Control-** The important thing here again is feeling. You do not have to be in control, but if your Lizard Brain/Baby Bear can fool itself into feeling in control, it will do so to avoid the same kinds of anxiety created by uncertainty.
• **The Need to Avoid Feeling Loss-** Whether it is loss of money, glory, prestige, power, affection or relationship, Baby Bear Brain/Lizard Brain **hates** this feeling.
• **The Need for Affiliation/Social Connection-** This need creates two particular phenomena. First-like attracts like. In business you tend to hire, consult with, collaborate with, and generally seek out people like you. It feels safe and predictably comfortable which keeps Baby Bear/Lizard Brain quiet. Secondly-people crave approval and social validation. Baby Bear/Lizard Brain loves the feeling of being part of the "in" crowd, and will put up quite a fight to avoid losing that feeling.

When our four basic needs are being challenged, the physical and psychic sensations are EQUIVALENT to the feelings our ancestors had when we were being chased by dinosaurs. Again, our brains cannot tell the difference between the two. Here is the catch: when we respond from Baby Bear/Lizard Brain we undermine the capacity to utilize the higher functioning part of our brains. The Pre-frontal Cortex (what I call our Human Brain or Papa Bear) operates in a completely different manner. It's conscious, slow, deliberate, and creative and has allowed our species to develop into artists, musicians, theologians, academicians, and doctors. Our Baby Bear/Lizard Brain seeks to meet those 4 basic needs at any and all costs (including abandonment of reasoned judgment). Instead of making measured, intentional decisions within the Papa Bear/Human Brain, Baby Bear overrides the Human Brain to get your four needs met the fastest and with the smallest amount of anxiety. This "dueling dual system" creates our Blind Spots.

So, What Are Cognitive Biases/Blind Spots?

They are best understood by some concrete examples of how behaviors associated with them:
• Not seeing the impact you have on others.
• Overestimating your strategic capabilities.
• Believing the rules don't apply to you.
• Avoiding difficult conversations.
• Having an answer for everything.
• Rationalizing poor performance by an underachieving hire.

They're a predictable pattern of errors in judgment, inferences about people and situations made in an illogical fashion. But at the same time we're absolutely certain that we are being logical, rational, and "right." Simply put, Blind Spots are built in thinking errors we make in processing information; largely due to conflict between the two systems we have hardwired in our heads- the Baby Bear 'Lizard Brain' and the Papa Bear 'Human Brain.' We are "predictably irrational". The concept of this 'dual process theory' is not new...but it is important to understand the biology behind it.

2 Myths about Blind Spots

Lest we believe that we can be inoculated from our cognitive biases, let's look at two common myths about Blind Spots. **Myth #1:** You can achieve a level of success and self-awareness where you no longer have Blind Spots. WRONG. Blind Spots are completely inescapable. No matter how good you get at recognizing your behavior patterns when you are operating out of your Blind Spots, or diffusing situations where your Blind Spots rear their ugly heads, you are HARD WIRED to make thinking errors based on what your Lizard Brain is telling you. *Myth #2:* I have already done a training that helped me see all my Blind Spots, so I am done. WRONG AGAIN. As new information becomes available and your circumstances shift, your Blind Spots will shift and change as well. The key is to be on the lookout for them so you can anticipate the errors in thinking that come from operating out of your Blind Spots.

The First Steps Towards Change

1. **Own it.** Have some healthy self-doubt. It is not weakness. It is not shameful. It is simply a part of life. The first step in making any meaningful change is the admission of the desire to do so. Understanding why Blind Spots exist and the underlying battle within your own brain goes a long way to that first step. 2. **Get a second opinion.** Judith Glaser, author of The DNA Of Leadership, says "Denial and Blind Spots are one of the primary reasons why Executive Coaching is so vital for leaders, and why peer coaching is equally important for employees to practice. Coaching can effectively uncover and deal with Blind Spots and denial and give the decision-makers a fresh perspective on how to handle executive challenges." Whether it is a peer group, a personal coach, friend, or spouse— be intellectually rigorous. Be hard on your opinions and decisions. Take them out and examine them thoroughly and intentionally. Have other people do the same, and never be afraid to make changes based on new data. Happy hunting!

APPENDIX B
BEHAVIORAL ECONOMICS

We do not consistently act in our own long-term self-interest. **Behavioral economics** is a hybrid discipline of psychology and economics that attempts to understand why this happens, and create systems for making better decisions.

Daniel Kahneman won the Nobel Prize for Economics but had a PhD in Psychology! He was the originator of Behavioral Economics in 1979.

Like many major breakthroughs, behavioral economics evolved from observation. Traditionally economists created models to predict how the ideal "Economic Man" would behave when making choices. *But, they didn't work!* Time and again, theorists were surprised that most people would consistently choose things that did not help them, and in some cases would behave in ways that were contrary to their own interests.

What emerged was the work of people like Kahneman, and later Dan Ariely who determined that people would behave in *predictably irrational* ways. Behavioral economics understands that human choices are prey to the quirks of human perception.

1. The Seductive Now

"I'll gladly pay tomorrow for a hamburger today." Wimpy

What happens NOW is of incredible importance to us as humans.

But we have a difficult time appropriately placing value on things that will happen in the future. This phenomenon is called *temporal discounting.*

Why it matters: The Real Time Detrimental Effects

Put numbers to it and this becomes increasingly clear. We all attach values to behaviors, so picking arbitrary numbers allows us to track this in a tangible way. For example: I know that starting an exercise program will be valuable- it will bring me, say, 8 units of value in the future. It requires an immediate cost of 6 units, which leaves a potential *future* gain of only 2 units. Starting tomorrow decreases both costs and benefits by half (to 4 and 3)... which results in an assumed *immediate* gain of 1 unit. OF COURSE EVERYONE IS ENTHUSIASTIC ABOUT GOING TO THE GYM *TOMORROW*!

EXAMPLES:

1. Failing to save money
2. Failing to exercise
3. Failing to join 401K matching programs
4. Mismanaging diabetes
5. Sex, Drugs, and Rock and Roll (Enough said)
6. Low enrollment in organ donor programs

2. The Relativity of Comparisons (The Decoy Effect)

We are hard wired to compare and contrast. It is built in to how we experience the world around us. But we focus on comparing things that are most easily comparable (A-A^1). We avoid comparing things that differ greatly (A-B).

Why it matters: The Real Time Detrimental Effects.

As decision-makers we are susceptible to being manipulated by the presence of these decoys. We make illogical judgments merely because we unconsciously take the easier path. (We go for *efficiency over effectiveness*.)

"Relativity helps us make decisions in life. But it can also make us downright miserable. Why? Because jealousy and envy spring from comparing our lot in life with that of others." –Dan Ariely, PhD

APPENDIX C
MINDFULNESS AND MEDITATION

What: Mindfulness is an attitude, stance, or posture of focused attention. Meditation is an exercise designed to help that attitude become more automatic.

Why do we need to do this? Often, instead of paying attention to the present moment (where everything is taking place), we create and inhabit a world between our ears. We participate in imagined conversations, re-live permutations of things that happened in the past, or anticipate what's going to happen in the future. Our brains cannot differentiate between what's going on in real time and what's going on between our ears. Thus, we become reactive. *Reacting to our thoughts and feelings, we're in a constant state of stress, anxiety, or anticipation.*

"The internal chatter of our minds is like having a roommate who won't stop talking. If that roommate were a walking talking being, you would not last a day." –Michael Singer, PhD

Why does it matter? Having a meditation practice enables you to create a gap between your internal dialogue and your reaction to that dialogue.

Remember, your internal voice is not trustworthy. When you listen to that voice, you are experiencing your representation of reality- *but not reality itself.* The "I" who is always talking inside your head will NEVER BE CONTENT. Therefore, responding is useless. It leads to reactivity, wasted energy, Blind Spots, errors in judgment, and ultimately psychic exhaustion.

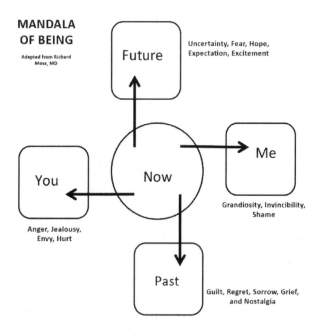

MANDALA OF BEING

Adapted from Richard Moss, MD

Future — Uncertainty, Fear, Hope, Expectation, Excitement

Me — Grandiosity, Invincibility, Shame

You — Anger, Jealousy, Envy, Hurt

Past — Guilt, Regret, Sorrow, Grief, and Nostalgia

Now

These negative emotions are not the problem...but are signals of the manner in which our minds have left the present.

"Meditation is the practice of using your attention on purpose to rid yourself of this inner troublemaker." -Michael Singer, PhD

How:

1. Meditation summarized

- Find a quiet place with minimal distractions
- Sit comfortably, making sure your knees are below your hips
- Lightly rest your palms on your knees
- Keep your eyes open, and focus your gaze 3-5 feet in front of you in a downward direction
- Pay attention to your breath
- Notice that you are talking to yourself
- Acknowledge that you are talking to yourself, internally say the word thinking
- Return focus to your breath

2. That internal voice is never content, never quiet, and always present. It is like having a roommate that NEVER SHUTS UP. Name the roommate (me):

Organizer	Reviewer
Planner	Processor
Pleaser	Evaluator
Victim	Rationalizer
Complainer	Rehearser
Critic	Rebellious Adolescent
Hero	Benevolent Father
Know it All	Healer
Self-Justifier	

The stories that your "roommate" tells you are flawed. When you make decisions based upon her advice, or based upon her perspective, you are vulnerable to be reactive, and make errors in judgment.

APPENDIX D
GRATITUDE AND THE BRAIN

I (KK) was infuriated with my assistant. My wife was making me crazy. My colleagues were insufferable. It was just one of those weeks where nothing went smoothly. For the third time in a row I heard my inner voice explode, "These people are all idiots!" Confession? When I am struggling, I see idiocy around me because my brain is looking for it. The brain is a wonderful thing...it will find proof for what it already believes is true. (Known in the biz as *confirmation bias*.) Fortunately, over time I have become more effective at recognizing this pattern. And as I am the only common link between the people irritating the shit out of me-I may be the problem.

The good news here? By simply reframing my interior monologue, I can make my confirmation bias work for me. By cultivating an attitude of gratitude, I can utilize my brain's inherent ability to see what it wants to see. Understanding the very real effect gratitude has on both your brain and your body can enable you to be much more effective, happy, and productive.

Okay. When I start talking about gratitude what images come to mind? (Longhaired hippies in a circle singing Kumbaya, Mystic gurus teaching the path to enlightenment, right?)

It is tempting to dismiss the idea of gratitude as fluff, or new-agey hokum, but that would be a huge mistake.

In fact, the measurable benefit of gratitude is based in hard science. There have been multiple studies utilizing functional MRI's and brain imaging techniques to map the effect of gratitude on the brain. And the effects are significant!

Gratitude affects our brains in two ways:

- *Biologic:* Researchers found dramatically increased activity in the hypothalamus when subjects were asked to evoke feelings of gratitude. THIS IS IMPORTANT. The hypothalamus is responsible for many of the body's day-to-day functions. Increased activity there correlates to better self-care, less stress, and overall better health.
- *Cognitive:* When you focus on things to be thankful for and then see the effects of your gratitude, your brain automatically looks for more things to be grateful for. ("That felt good, I want more!") This is hijacking your brain's natural tendency toward confirmation bias to your advantage.

Personal and Professional Benefits of Gratitude

Gratitude affects every aspect of life. When you practice gratitude, the effects are far reaching. Most significantly? Cultivating a gratitude practice brings physical benefits, emotional and social benefits, and even career benefits.

- *Physical*: Remember that increased hypothalamus activity in the brain? Consistent gratitude can result in **better sleep, fewer aches and pains**, and more exercise (and those wonderful endorphins that accompany it.)
- *Emotional/Social*: In a recent article in *Psychology Today*, "Grateful Brain" researchers found that higher levels of gratitude are associated with **lower anxiety and depression**.

Simply ten minutes a day of focused time reflecting upon reasons to be grateful resulted in measurable differences in overall attitude.

- *Career:* "Gratitude makes you a more effective manager, helps you network, **increases your decision making**

capabilities, increases your productivity, and helps you get mentors and protégés. As a result, gratitude helps you achieve your career goals, as well as making your workplace a more friendly and enjoyable place to be."

Grateful people are attractive, charismatic. Networking comes easier and collaborative work is more readily accomplished. And when your physical health is improved you have the stamina to make good decisions even when the going gets tough.

What Hinders an Attitude of Gratitude?

Western culture is distinctly uncomfortable with gratitude. We pride ourselves on being 'self-made.' We perceive gratitude as weakness. Best advice? Get over it.

Common Beliefs About Gratitude:

- *Expressing gratitude is cheesy.* Well, yes. It can be. But here is the deal: Are you willing to miss out on the benefits of reflecting gratitude because of the 'risk' of being seen as corny? Sheesh, if there is benefit to being corny, why not give it a try?
- *Gratitude is for new-age hippies, not for me.* Being associated with a concept that has a touchy-feely vibe can feel risky. It can feel as if the cost is too high. Eleanor Roosevelt once said "Do what you feel in your heart to be right, for you'll be criticized anyway." If expressing gratitude has a measurable benefit to your brain, your body, and your business, it is for everyone.

3 Ways to Get Started

1. ***Start with a single thought***-When you wake up in the morning, think of one thing you are happy to have, one goal you achieved, one person you are grateful to know. Dwell on that thought for a few moments to start your

day. Keep it simple. You can even turn a common negative emotion around. Instead of 'I don't want to get up', make a slight grateful shift to "I am grateful for my extremely comfortable bed, and I love my new sheets." (Yeah, I can see your eyes rolling at that suggestion, but...) You will be amazed at the difference.

2. ***Keep a gratitude journal***-Humans are notoriously bad at accountability. Even with the best of intentions, if you merely think grateful thoughts you may not see any changes. At the end of every day make a quick note about something good that happened during the day. (Set yourself up for success- don't shoot for the moon! It does not have to be a novel, just a quick reminder to end the day with gratitude.)

3. ***Give praise*** –When you are grateful for someone's actions, be sure to tell them. In a funny way, this is fairly selfish. You actually end up reinforcing your own feelings of gratitude. Don't overthink it. Dominique Jones says, "The words you use have less impact than the tone you say them in." Just be specific and sincere.

Moral of the Story?

Let's get back to my week. I could tell you that I sat and reflected and everything miraculously shifted. Not *entirely* true. My assistant cried (and actually stomped her foot at me in my office). One of my colleagues noticed my malaise and commented on it. No comment about my wife. BUT, I was able to break free of the downward spiral MUCH more quickly than if I had continued to collect evidence of everyone's incompetency. And as an added bonus, I felt gratified by my ability to manipulate my pesky confirmation bias into working for me instead of against me.

Author Anais Nin wrote, "We do not see things as *they* are, we see things as *we* are." If you can remember to be grateful, the things you see will reflect that, and in the long run, you will be happier, healthier, and more productive for it.

APPENDIX E
INFLAMMATION AND THE BRAIN

We are in trouble. As a culture, we are sick. One in eight people suffer from clinical depression. Forty million people suffer from anxiety. Heart disease is the leading cause of death across ethnicities accounting for 1 in 4 deaths. Ten percent of Americans suffer from diabetes. Twenty percent of Americans suffer from autoimmune diseases like rheumatoid arthritis and lupus. We spend millions of dollars annually in treating and managing these diseases, but we are losing the battle. The common pathway to all this destruction? Chronic systemic inflammation inherited by our evolutionary forefathers.

We tend to separate mental health disorders from physical diseases like high blood pressure, heart disease, and diabetes. But if we want to understand the rising incidence of disease-both mental and physical- we need to look at the evolution of our bodies immune response to threats.

INFLAMMATION THEN (Caveman)

Early man was besieged by danger. We fought predators and the threat of physical harm. Fight or flight. Our bodies were equipped to adapt to those threats that challenged our survival. And it was supported primarily by an inflammatory response created by our immune system. Our immune systems fought against bacteria, viruses, cholera, the plague, polio, and measles. Our immune response was appropriate to the threat. When we got infections, our bodies reacted with inflammation. We got fevers, we experienced pain, and we became immobile. We acted sick. We retreated. We slept. We hunkered down and allowed our bodies to fight the fight for us.

INFLAMMATION NOW (CEO)

Today, we live in a relatively sterilized environment. For the most part, we no longer battle threats to physical safety (in the guise of predators or bacteria) on a daily basis. But here is where things get complicated. To modern man, social threats look NO different than the physical threats of our prehistoric predecessors. Conflict at the office, boardroom drama, bankruptcy, divorce, political discourse, and religious conflict all contribute to what researchers call psychosocial stress. Our primitive bodies perceive these modern psychosocial stressors as deadly threats. The perceived danger signals our bodies to initiate an inflammatory response akin to predators chasing us down. Physically and psychologically it is the same fight or flight response that the Cave Man experienced. We may have evolved in many ways, but not in our body's response to danger. Rather than focus on the details of the immeasurably complex human immune system, let's keep it simple.

Our bodies are predisposed to react to ANY threat (real or imagined) with an inflammatory response.

At its core, the system works like this:

1. External or internal stimuli acts as threats to the system. (Stress)
2. The sympathetic and parasympathetic nervous system responds. (Release the hounds! Marshal the troops! Fight!)
3. The body produces increased numbers of stress hormones and white blood cells. Those cells then trigger the brain to produce an inflammatory response. (Your body sets your brain on fire.)
4. Modern stimuli are overwhelming our immune systems. More specifically? The deeply ingrained, genetic predisposition to respond to threats with inflammation is constantly activated by the modern world. You've heard

the expression 'all dressed up with no place to go?' That is us. Our inflammatory response to psychosocial, dietary, and environmental stressors is ultimately damaging and toxic to our physical and mental health.

WHY

Chronic states of inflammation lead to chronic disease. Inflammatory compounds have a direct impact on the brain's ability to properly utilize neurotransmitters. What? In laymen's terms, when your brain is inflamed it is difficult to regulate your mood. Inflamed brain= higher likelihood of depression, anxiety, and mood disorders. So the boardroom argument that triggers the same inflammatory response that resulted in fight or flight, now results in a state of constant anxiety. Look at the behaviors demonstrated by depressed individuals. Sleeping, retreating, withdrawal. Depressed people also often report more sensitivity to pain. (What did our ancestors do when they were sick with the plague or cholera?) Filing for bankruptcy signals the body to produce an inflammatory response. Without a clear 'enemy' the brain stays inflamed, and the sickness behaviors appear without the infection. The president of the company holes up in his home. Sleeps all day (hypersomnia). Ignores phone calls (isolation) and feels terrible (anhedonia). What we all recognize today as depression. The bad news does not end there. Chronic inflammation not only has profound effects in the brain but also goes on to affect the rest of the body. Increased production of stress hormones like cortisol leads to weight gain. Imbalance in pancreatic hormone production yields diabetes. The list goes on and on.

NEXT

There is hope. There are ways to mitigate the effects of stress on our bodies. Not surprisingly, it is the usual suspects! (Our eating habits, exercise, and sleep really do matter.)

Unfortunately, we can all get lost in the details and get overwhelmed. We tell ourselves "That is a really good idea. I will start it tomorrow." Then we never actually do it. Such is the paradox of being human!

So, we're going to provide actionable checkpoints to get started NOW with reengineering your body and brain's response to modern life.

APPENDIX F
LAB TESTS FOR COGNITIVE HEALTH

A college coed's fatigue and lack of concentration seem like depression but signal a thyroid imbalance that medication can correct. A middle aged CEO has his first episode of depression. Apathetic, with loss of mental clarity, he was diagnosed with diabetes and high blood pressure. An ex-football player complained of chronic pain and anxiety. He was deficient in vitamin B12, folate, and vitamin D. Turns out he was drinking excessively to treat his pain. The resultant vitamin deficiencies actually made his pain and irritability worse.

More than 100 medical disorders masquerade as mental illness. Medical conditions may cause 25% of mental health issues. With chronic inflammation being a common element in depression, diabetes, heart disease, anxiety, and thyroid disease, it is important to get laboratory tests.

Lab work (in addition to a thorough clinical interview) is essential to rule out medical conditions pretending to be depression. Looking for markers of inflammation, evaluating the thyroid gland, and checking for common vitamin deficiencies, it is possible to quickly hone in on medical causes. Laboratory tests can be overwhelming in both quantity and complexity, so here is a list of essential labs. By no means a complete list, it is a significant start to making dramatic improvement in healing and living.

Thyroid Function Tests: The thyroid is essential for the body's metabolism, use of energy, and control of other hormones. Thyroid deficiencies are a leading cause of brain fog, lethargy, fatigue, depression, and cognitive impairments. Hashimoto's is the most common hypothyroid illness seen in women. It is an autoimmune disease where the body attacks the thyroid gland leading to thyroid deficiency. Most physicians will merely get a thyroid screening test called the TSH or thyroid-stimulating hormone. However, too often hypothyroidism, particularly

Hashimoto's, is missed. Therefore, I recommend the following battery of thyroid function tests that together give a complete picture of the thyroid glands ability to help us maintain good cognitive health.

TSH- thyroid stimulating hormone
Free T4- inactive form of the thyroid hormone
Free T3- active form of the thyroid hormone
Reverse T3- is elevated with bodily stress as a means of slowing down and conserving energy for recovery from stress
Thyroid peroxidase antibodies- elevated in Hashimoto's
Thyroglobulin antibodies- elevated in Hashimoto's

Vitamin B12: Vitamin B12 is a basic building block of life. It makes red blood cells, nerve cell lining, and aids in other brain functions. It protects the nervous system and regulates mood cycles. Deficiency leads to depression, memory loss, and confusion. In fact, 40% of the population is deficient because of poor diet, malabsorption, and diabetes drugs.

Highly Sensitive C-reactive protein: C-reactive protein is elevated with general or systemic inflammation. Remember, inflammation is the primary cause of brain fog, depression, and anxiety. Cardiologists have long used highly sensitive C-reactive protein as a screening test for cardiovascular risk. C-reactive protein is also a useful marker for depression risk and brain inflammation.

Vitamin B9 (folate): Folate is one of many essential vitamins needed for copying and synthesizing DNA, producing new cells, and supporting nerve and immune functions.

Homocysteine: Homocysteine is an inflammatory protein metabolized by vitamin B12 and folic acid. When elevated, it is an indication that B12 is deficient. Cardiologists also use it as an indicator of cardiovascular risk. Homocysteine is an amino acid thought to damage the lining of your arteries and other cells of the body, including the brain.

Fasting glucose/fasting insulin/hemoglobin A1c: Elevated blood sugar is one of the biggest risk factors for general inflammation leading to depression and brain fog. Hemoglobin A1c shows the average of blood sugar levels over the last 90 days (the lifespan of a red blood cell).

Serum 25-OH Vitamin D: This is one of the most common vitamin deficiencies found in my medical practice. In fact, just yesterday I met with a profoundly depressed 20-year-old who had a vitamin D level of 7. The normal range is 50-80! Vitamin D3 lowers blood sugar, blood pressure, cholesterol and inflammation. It helps metabolize hormones, improves mood, and reduces the risk of many cancers, heart disease and autoimmune disease. It also boosts your immune system during the winter months. Vitamin D3 turns on genes that keep you from being inflamed.

ALT (alanine aminotransferase): Nonalcoholic fatty liver disease is the most common cause of ALT elevation. Nonalcoholic fatty liver disease is seen with insulin resistance, obesity, and systemic inflammation. Elevated ALT is associated with depression and is used as an independent marker showing risk of developing depression.

Comprehensive metabolic profile: A comprehensive metabolic profile is a screening test to show function of the liver, kidneys, electrolytes, and blood sugar. It is a quick and dirty overview of major body systems that ultimately affect the brain and cognition. CBC with differential: Anemia is a common feature of depression and fatigue. Vitamin B12, iron, and folate deficiencies are the most common causes of anemia. Additionally the CBC demonstrates evidence of infection and stress.

MTHFR: The MTHFR tests for a defect in the genes that are responsible for methylation. Methylation is an essential biologic process that controls everything from your stress response and how your body makes energy from food, to your brain chemistry and detoxification. Those with an MTHFR mutation are at risk for poor enzyme efficiency. Consequently, folate and folic acid cannot be efficiently converted into their active form, known as 5-MTHF or L-methylfolate. Therefore those nutrients can't perform one of their key functions: breaking down (recycling) Homocysteine. Homocysteine is naturally formed in the body, but gets broken down (recycled) by 5-MTHF, reducing the incidence of inflammation.

Magnesium (RBC): Magnesium is a mineral responsible for many functions including energy production in the cells, reaction to stress, and "calming" of the brain and nervous system.
Magnesium deficiencies are prevalent in depression, anxiety, and sleep issues.

Iron profile including serum ferritin: Iron-deficiency anemia is caused by a lack of iron. Anemia is defined as a decrease in the number of red blood cells or the amount of hemoglobin in the blood. When anemia comes on slowly, the symptoms are often vague and may include feeling tired, weakness, shortness of breath or poor ability to exercise.

APPENDIX G
IMPROVE COGNITIVE HEALTH
BEST SUPPLEMENTS

As recently as ten years ago, depression was exclusively labeled as a chemical imbalance in the brain and treated as such. We know better now, and we are striving to do better. The generally held concept of depression as a "chemical imbalance" has essentially been debunked. Rather than an imbalance of serotonin, dopamine, or norepinephrine (neurotransmitters), depression and anxiety actually begin further up the chain of events in our brains. Depression is more directly linked to effects of chronic inflammation on the brain. Thus, the emphasis is shifting. Instead of only antidepressants (SSRI, SNRI, TCAs), we are including adjunctive use of supplements to decrease brain inflammation.

The research currently being done supports this claim. A paper published in the American Journal of Psychiatry June 1, 2016 concluded that there was strong evidence to support adjunctive use of SAMe, methylfolate, Omega-3, and vitamin D with antidepressants to reduce depressive symptoms.

My 35 years of clinical experience (KK) has supported these findings, so I will share my recommendations for supplements to protect your brain much like a cardiologist protects the heart from the effects of inflammation. As with our heart, it's more important to treat the root cause of anxiety and depression- *inflammation of the brain*- than just the symptoms.

There are a lot of options for supplements. To simplify the process, I broke my recommendations down into 5 core basics, and a list of additional supplements to consider.

THE 5 CORE BASICS

1. METHYLFOLATE:

Methylfolate is a B vitamin, and it supports the brain and aids in manufacturing DNA, neurotransmitters, and removal of cellular waste products. Methylfolate stabilizes our mood through its role in neurotransmitter synthesis and production. Patients taking 15 mg per day showed significant improvement in response rate and the degree of change in their depression scores as compared to SSRI therapy plus placebo.

Methylfolate is the most biologically available form of folate, AKA folic acid. Forty percent (40%!!) of people can't absorb regular folate because of a genetic mutation in their MTHFR gene (methylenetetrahydrofolate reductase), which prevents absorption of regular folate. There is a blood test to confirm the genetic mutation, but I do not require it. I recommend Methylfolate for all patients who need folate, regardless of the presence of mutation. So what is the benefit of the blood test? Some insurance companies will reimburse for purchase of methylfolate in the presence of this genetic mutation.

The daily recommended dose is 7.5 mg to 15 mg daily.

Which ones:

Deplin 15 mg (http://www.deplin.com)

5-MTHF 15 mg   Thorne Research

2. VITAMIN D3:

Vitamin D3 is basically a neuro-steroid. Vitamin D receptors reside in areas of the brain involved with depression. Vitamin D assists the body with making neurotransmitters, decreasing stress response, and ultimately reducing inflammation in the body and the brain. I see Vitamin D3 deficiency most commonly in my practice and 75% of the US teen and adult population is deficient in vitamin D. People with vitamin D levels below 20 had an 85% increased risk of depression than those whose levels were higher than 30!

Laboratory testing is necessary for proper monitoring of vitamin D3 treatment and replacement. I attempt to maintain levels of 35 to 60. It is possible to overdo vitamin D supplements, so I strongly urge you to establish the dosages based on the lab values of (25)-

hydroxy vitamin D. Repeat the lab three months after initiation of vitamin D3 supplements to make sure you are within appropriate limits. With that said, 2000 international units daily is a reasonable starting dose but make sure to retest to ensure proper dosing.

The daily recommended dose to initiate vitamin D3 supplementation is 2000 international units a day. 5000-10000 iU may be necessary to treat D3 deficiency but make sure you follow up with your prescribing doctor.

Which ones:

Pure Encapsulations

Thorne Research – Vitamin D/K2 Liquid

3. OMEGA-3 FATTY ACIDS:

The majority of American diets lack healthy fats including the Omega-3 fatty acids. Cardiologists have long recommended Omega-3s for their role in overall heart health because of their strong anti-inflammatory properties. They have now become a cornerstone in maintaining brain and mental health. A recent meta-analysis demonstrated significant reduction in depression beyond placebo with the use of Omega-3 fatty acids.

If you take no other supplements for your mental and cognitive health the Omega-3s are an absolute must!

Omega-3s are essential for fighting inflammation. Again, inflammation is the central contributor to depression, anxiety, diabetes, obesity, heart disease, cancer, and autoimmune diseases.

There are three Omega-3s: EPA (Eicosapentaenoic Acid), DHA (Docosahexaenoic Acid), and ALA (Alpha-linolenic Acid). We find EPAs and DHAs in animal based fats and ALAs are plant based, found in foods like nuts and flaxseed. Although beneficial for general health, ALAs are not effective as an adjunct therapy for depression and anxiety. For mental health, EPA dominant formulas are essential as DHA alone is not effective. An omega-3 formula with a 2:1 to 5:1 ratio of EPA to DHA is recommended.

The best sources of omega-3's are from wild Alaskan salmon, sardines, skipjack tuna, and anchovies. There is the risk of foreign contaminants like PCPs and mercury in seafood. Small fish such as sardines and anchovies are less likely to contain contaminants and high quality fish oil is specifically filtered and distilled to eliminate them. Fish oil supplements are the next best source.

Be aware that there can be side effects of long-term supplementation including increased bleeding. (So be cautious if you are taking blood thinners etc., and make sure you let your Doctor know what supplements you are on.)

My daily recommended dose is 1500 mg to 2000 mg per day with depression and anxiety. Higher doses can be used effectively for bipolar disorder.

Which ones:

Nordic Naturals

Central Market Store Brand

Whole Foods Store Brand

Kirkland Store Brand

4. B-COMPLEX WITH MINERALS:

Low levels of B vitamins are associated with mood disorders. The brain needs high amounts of B vitamins in order to repair and maintain neurotransmitter function. Stress depletes B vitamins quickly. Additionally, these vitamins are needed for healthy hair, skin, adrenal function, liver function, and to help the nervous system. The B vitamins include B1 (thiamine), B2 (riboflavin), B3 (niacin), B6 (pyridoxine), B9 (folate), vitamin B12, biotin, and B5 (pantothenic acid). Minerals such as magnesium, zinc, iodine, and selenium are necessary for the body's maximum function.

Which ones:

MultiThera1 with Vit K by Prothera

5. PROBIOTICS:

Probiotics are "good" bacteria that have significant anti-inflammatory effects. Strains of bifidobacterium and lactobacillus have shown to decrease depressive symptoms. We are only beginning to understand the role of the "gut-brain" axis and the links between good gastro-intestinal health and the maintenance of good mental health and overall well-being. In fact there was a recent study that showed a link to OCD and the gut microbiome (bacteria).

Which Ones:
Ther-Biotic by Klaire Labs
Prescript Assist

ADDITIONAL SUPPLEMENTS FOR CONSIDERATION
SAMe:
Like folate, SAMe assists the body in the production of neurotransmitters. It has been available in Europe by prescription since the 1970s for treatment of depression. In a 2013 U.S. study, people who took SAMe regularly showed significant decreases in depression rating scales and only a 36% incidence of remission. Be aware! There have been some reports of irritability with use and it may cause hypomania in those with bipolar disorder.

Tryptophan or 5 – HTTP:
5-HTTP is an amino acid that is a precursor to the neurotransmitter serotonin. The overall evidence of its usefulness in treating depression doesn't seem to be all that robust. Use caution when you take this with a prescription antidepressant as it can cause dangerous side effects called serotonin syndrome. I do not prescribe this to patients already taking antidepressants.

Magnesium:
We see magnesium deficiency in 80% of depressed individuals and magnesium plays an important role in anxiety by disrupting the body's stress response systems.
The recommended dose is 150-800 mg per day. If you are using magnesium to treat anxiety, irritability, insomnia, or premenstrual symptoms, start at 300 mg per day. I prefer magnesium glycinate unless there's a problem with constipation. Magnesium oxide or magnesium citrate can provide a laxative effect for some.

Zinc:
Zinc is a mineral essential for controlling the body's reaction and response to stress. Zinc deficiency leads to symptoms of depression, difficulties with memory and learning, and even aggression.
Recommended dose is 15 to 30 mg per day.

L-Theanine:
L-theanine is an amino acid that has a calming effect by triggering the release of GABA. It is found primarily in green tea and enhances alpha wave production, which promotes a relaxed but focused mindset.
Recommended dose is 100 to 200 mg twice per day.

Curcumin:
Curcumin, found in the spice turmeric has known anti-inflammatory and neuro-protective properties. Recent studies have shown its effectiveness in treating depression.
Recommended dose: 1000 mg curcumin extract daily
Which one: Meriva 500 SF (Soy Free) By Thorne

This is by no means a comprehensive list. Before starting any supplementation regimen, it is important to consult with your physician. You may also wish to order diagnostic blood work to determine appropriate dosage.

APPENDIX H
WHAT IS IMPOSTER SYNDROME?

All too often, highly accomplished people walk around feeling like imposters. Truth be told, I (KK) feel that way occasionally. Recently, I was talking with two friends and realized we had each faced decisions where our initial response was to feel overwhelmed, under-prepared, and generally fraudulent. Meet Christine and Steven-my two friends.

Christine recently accepted a new VP position and it was a great step for her. She had been courted by the CEO, offered a salary increase (to the tune of 40%!) and asked to take on exciting responsibilities. Yet, she was miserable. When she talked about this new opportunity, several things emerged.

Christine felt that asking questions about things she did not know or understand would weaken the initial impression her CEO and team had of her. Somehow, she believed that she was expected to already "know" the answers. Even early in her new position, colleagues experienced her as distant and aloof. She seemed to want to 'fly solo' instead of being the team player they were expecting.

At first pass, Steven was in a different place. Historically successful as an entrepreneur, he was filling every spare second of his time accruing training, certifications, and degrees. His professional life was effectively on 'hold' while he continued to seek more educational trophies.

Both Christine and Steven were experiencing variations of Imposter Syndrome.

Imposter syndrome can be broken down into a few key components. Those who suffer from Imposter Syndrome:

- Are unable to recognize their accomplishments.
- Dismiss success as due to luck, good timing, or deceit.
- Feel as if they have misrepresented themselves, or have been misrepresented.
- Think their CEOs over-estimate their ability, knowledge, or skill.

They are afraid of being seen as an Imposter, a Poser, or a Fraud.

YOU ARE NOT ALONE! Imposter Syndrome is epidemic amongst physicians, lawyers, executives, and impacts 7 out of 10 professional people.

Effects of Imposter Syndrome

Let's break this down a bit further. Examine the diagram below. The left image represents how people suffering from Imposter Syndrome see the world. The right image is more in keeping with the way the world really is. Both Christine and Steven (and I) were stuck on the left side of this diagram. EVEN THOUGH her CEO had confidence in her, her work spoke for itself, and she had superior skills, **Christine was unable to see the positive things she brought to the table.**

Christine could only see her inadequacies. And because she wanted to hide them, she did not ask questions. Because she did not ask questions, she did not engage with her colleagues. (Do you see where this is headed?) The Christine they hired was a confident and competent team player. The Christine showing up was distant, not engaged, and aloof. In order to protect herself, Christine had unwittingly created a bigger problem.

Steven was addressing this skewed perspective slightly differently. Instead of trying to camouflage his perceived inadequacy, he was stuck trying to enlarge his 'circle' of knowledge. He was in a place of paralysis; attempting to learn everything about everything before taking his next step professionally.

Do You Have Imposter Syndrome?

If 7/10 people suffer from Imposter Syndrome, odds are that it affects you. How can you tell? Let's go through a quick checklist:

- Do you feel disappointed in your accomplishments?
- Do you find it difficult to complete a project as well as you would like to?
- Are you worried that your colleagues will find out how much knowledge or skill you lack?
- Do you think you give the impression that you are more able than you actually are?
- Do you worry about living up to your peers' expectations?
- Do you routinely compare your ability to those around you and feel lacking in skill, intelligence or success?
- Do you expect to routinely perform flawlessly and with ease?

Do you have more yes's than no's? If so, you have Imposter Syndrome.

The more successful, intelligent, and accomplished you are the MORE likely you are to suffer occasional bouts of feeling like a fraud.

5 Steps to Combat Imposter Syndrome

1. **STOP SEEKING PERFECTION.** Perfectionism is one of the most detrimental personality traits around. Successful people hold themselves to a high standard but perfection is too high a standard. "Lower your standards of perfection. You don't

have to attain perfection to be worthy of the success you've achieved. If you continually set the bar at a level of perfection, you will *always* feel disappointed. Set the bar at a realistic level so that you don't always fall short, " says Lauren Feiner, PsyD.

2. **OWN IT.** The first step in gaining any sort of clarity about what you face is owning it. Find one person to confide in. Say out loud "I feel like a fraud." It may sound silly but getting it out into the open makes it much easier to gain perspective.

3. **PAY ATTENTION TO YOUR STRENGTHS.** You have assets. List them. Actually write them out and refer back to them when you are feeling inept. Learn how to take a compliment. Simply say thanks, and reflect upon the good work you have done.

4. **GATHER A TRIBE.** Surround yourself with smart people. Accept help. You can't save your face and your ass at the same time! So be bold-acknowledge when you need help and accept it when it is offered to you.

5. **ACKNOWLEDGE YOUR LIMITATIONS.** No one is perfect. No one can know everything about everything. The sooner you make peace with that, the better off you will be.

Make a Plan-It's Not the End of the World

Maya Angelou was one of the most renowned authors of our time. She was also quite transparent about her own battles with Imposter Syndrome: "I have written eleven books, but each time I think, 'Uh oh, they're going to find out now. I've run a game on everybody, and they're going to find me out.'"

Imposter Syndrome does not have to derail you. Both Christine and Steven are successful people. The root of the challenges they face is Imposter Syndrome. But they now have a playbook for future action and are on the lookout for that pesky little voice in the back of their head telling them they are undeserving of their success.

APPENDIX I
COMPELLING WHY

Your "compelling why" is the deeper motivation and inspiration behind why you make the decisions you do. Why are you an accountant and not an artist? Why do you choose to live in Texas rather than Washington?

Your "compelling why" should be in the background, if not at the forefront, of all your business development strategies, tactics, and actions. At its core, the compelling why is simply the articulation of your motivating factors. Although this exercise is worded in terms of the motivations behind career decisions, the same rules apply for personal decision-making. Why do you want to change? What is motivating you to seek out a new home/hobby/lifestyle/relationship?

For most people, your professional "compelling why" originates, at least consciously, from one of two places:

1. You suffered a trauma of some sort, physically, mentally, or emotionally, that you've overcome or found ways to deal with. And one of the ways you heal that trauma and transcend the pain is to help others to either avoid that trauma or make it easier for them to deal with it.
2. You experienced some kind of uplifting experience or transformation, and you feel compelling to share that kind of experience with others.

Your personal 'compelling why' may be motivated by similar experiences or may stem from your personal history, habits or culture.

Your "compelling why" is one element that goes into telling a bigger picture story about who you are and what you stand for.

The simplest approach for crafting your "compelling why" is to answer questions about the forces that shaped you throughout your lifetime and identify any significant turning points, events, or experiences. From your responses to these questions, you'll have the raw material to craft a description about what inspires and compels you to do the work you do, and to make the decisions you make.

STEP 1: The Forces That Shaped You:
- Did you experience any traumatic experiences that inspired you to do the work that you do now? Describe them.
- Did you experience any positive, life-altering experiences that affected you deeply? Describe them.
- What people influenced you positively?
- What people had a negative influence on you?
- From these experiences, what did you see or recognize that was wrong (or right) and, therefore, felt called to do something about?

STEP 2: Turning Points, Events, and Experiences:
Can you identify when and where you decided to do the work you do now?

STEP 3: Write a brief description about what inspires and compels you to do the work you do.

Example:

I spent the better part of my early adulthood in the pursuit of education and the accumulation of knowledge. I majored in Mathematics in college. After medical school came time as a public health physician working in rural Texas, followed by Board Certification in Emergency Medicine. The ability to fly by the seat of my pants in the face of life-threatening trauma and illness excited me. I was damned good, or so I thought, at keeping the emotional 'spillage' at a distance. Young and full of testosterone, I pushed myself; working 25 days (or more) every month, year after year. I ignored the extra 20lbs, chronic insomnia, and increasing isolation. I prided myself on being smart, educated, and a facts and data guy. But 'shift' happened. I crashed into the proverbial wall. A new word entered into my lexicon- vicarious traumatization. I had not appreciated the personal cost of watching others suffer while ignoring my own self-care. Forced by the reality of professional burnout, it was unrealistic to continue as I had.

After taking a year off digging trenches for my septic system (insert shit story here), and building rock walls, I came to terms with how bereft and befuddled I truly was. How unbalanced towards the mental/thinking quadrant I was. Retraining as a psychiatrist and psychoanalyst, I began to integrate all of the quadrants of my life and now work with more discernable balance and efficacy. That journey inspires me to help other 'stuck' people get 'unstuck'.

APPENDIX J
CORE VALUES

Essential to the cultivation and maintenance of spiritual resilience, it is imperative that you be clear and declarative about your own personal values.

Knowing your values provides a beacon and compass to guide you in your decision-making. When you make decisions that are in alignment with your core values, you are in the 'sweet spot of resilience'.

Review this list and choose 10 of these values that resonate with you. After choosing them, write a mission statement,

"I promise to live a life of... (Place Value Here)."

When making a decision, you can refer to your mission statement asking yourself if this decision is in alignment with your core values.

Here is a list of core values to begin your exercise.

	Beauty	Country,
Abundance	Belonging	Patriotism
Acceptance	Calm	Courage
Accomplishment	Challenge	Creativity
Achievement	Change	Curiosity
Accountability	Charisma	Decisiveness
Accuracy	Contribution	Delight of being
Advancement	Commitment	Dependability
Adventure	Community	Diligence
Affection	Competence	Discipline
Affluence	Comfort	Discovery
Arts	Compassion	Duty
Authenticity	Competition	Education
Autonomy	Contribution	Effectiveness
Awareness	Cooperation	Efficiency
Balance	Coordination	Empowerment

Equality
Ethical practice
Excellence
Excitement
Expansion
Fairness
Faith
Fame
Family
Fast living
Financial gain
Fitness
Flair
Freedom
Friendships
Fun
Generosity
Giving
Gratitude
Growth
Harmony
Health
Helping others
Holiness
Honesty
Honor
Hope
Humility
Humor
Independence
Individuality,
Influencing
Ingenuity

Inner harmony
Inner peace
Innovation
Inspiration
Integrity
Intellectual
Intensity
Intimacy
Involvement
Joy
Justice
Kindness
Knowledge
Leadership
Learning
Logic
Love
Loyalty
Morality
Orderliness
Partnership
Passion
Patience
Peace
Peace of mind
Perfection
Perseverance
Play
Pleasure
Power
Practicality
Privacy
Production

Progress
Prosperity
Public service
Punctuality
Purity
Purpose
Quality
Relationships
Respect
Responsibility
Reverence
Safety
Security
Self-expression
Strength
Succulence
Success
Spirituality
Teamwork
Tolerance
Transformation
Truth
Unstoppable
Wealth
Well-being
Wisdom

"I promise to live a life of…"

APPENDIX K
GOLDILOCKS METHOD

The Goldilocks Method for Understanding Resilience			
	Too Much Stress/Stimulation	"Just Right" Resilience Sweet Spot	Not Enough Too Much Recovery
Physical		CDC- ability to carry out daily tasks with vigor and alertness, no undue fatigue, with ample energy to enjoy leisure and respond to emergency	
	Injury		Atrophy
	Impairment		Weakness
	Pain		Exhaustion
	Overuse		Disease
Spiritual	Hyper-Religiosiy	Clarity of Values	Loss of purpose
	Judgement	Sense of Connection	Existentially Lost
	Fundamentalism	Belonging to something	Loss of Meaning
	Legalism	bigger than oneself (Community, Family, God)	Lethargy
Mental	Errors in Judgment	Focus	Indecisive
	Rigidity	Creativity	Foggy thinking
	Inflexibility of thinking	Freshness	Low risk tolerance
	Impulsivity	Risk Tolerant	Avoidance
	Cognitive Closure	Clarity	
Emotional	Irritability	Self aware	Depression
	Anxiety	Understand how emotions	Apathy
	Projection	affect others, and how	Withdrawal
	Anger	their emotions affect you	Social Isolation
	Easily Frustrated	Joyful and Content	

APPENDIX L
FEELINGS WORDS JOURNAL EXERCISE

To increase your self awareness of your emotions and feelings, it is essential to broaden your feelings vocabulary. Most of us, especially men, know when we are 'hungry, horny, or pissed', but are at a loss to explain nuances of emotions, which is essential for Emotional Intelligence.

We recommend keeping a daily journal for a month and recording three affective or emotional words that you experienced that day. Over time, you'll get more fluent at describing your emotional experiences and reactions.

Here's a list to look at as you record in your journal- think of it as an emotional translator. As humans, when we have words to describe our internal experience, we grow more capable of real time analysis of our emotional reactions.

"Today, I felt _____, when _____."
"Today, I felt _____, when _____."
"Today, I felt _____, when _____."

acceptance	anticipation	cheer	cruelty
adoration	anxiety	closeness	curiosity
affection	apathy	comfort	defeat
agitation	appreciation	compassion	delight
agony	apprehension	competence	dejection
alarm	arousal	completion	depression
alertness	arrogance	composure	desire
alienation	aversion	concern	despair
amazement	bewilderment	confidence	detachment
ambivalence	bitterness	confusion	determination
amusement	boldness	constraint	disappointment
anger	boredom	contempt	discovery
angst	bravery	contentment	disgust
anguish	calm	courage	dismay
annoyance	caution	cowardice	disrespect

distance
distress
dread
ecstasy
elan
elation
embarrassment
empathy
emptiness
ennui
envy
euphoria
exasperation
excitement
exhaustion
expectation
familiarity
fear
ferocity
fondness
freedom
friendship
fright
frustration
fury
gaiety
gain
generosity
gladness
glee
gloom
gratitude
greed
grief
grouchiness
grumpiness
guilt
happiness

hatred
honor
hope
horror
humiliation
humility
hysteria
impatience
inadequacy
incompetence
incompleteness
indecision
independence
indifference
infatuation
innocence
insecurity
inspiration
intent
interest
ire
irritability
isolation
jealousy
joy
jolliness
jubilation
kindness
lack
leniency
limerence
loathing
loneliness
longing
loss
love
lust
melancholy

misery
modesty
mortification
negativity
neglect
nervousness
nostalgia
obligation
optimism
outrage
pain
panic
paranoia
passion
pathos
patience
peace
pity
pleasure
pride
purity
puzzlement
rage
rapture
rashness
regret
relief
reluctance
remorse
repentance
repose
repulsion
resentment
resistance
respect
revulsion
sadness
satisfaction

schadenfreude
scorn
security
self-pity
serenity
shame
shock
shyness
sorrow
spite
stress
suffering
surprise
suspense
suspicion
sympathy
tenderness
terror
thrills
timidity
togetherness
tolerance
torment
triumph
understanding
unhappiness
vengefulness
vulnerability
warmth
weariness
woe
wonder
worry
wrath
yearning
zeal
zest

APPENDIX M
RESOURCES FOR FURTHER STUDY

BOOKS:
- *Crucial Conversations: Tools For Talking When Stakes Are High, Patterson*, Grenny, McMillan, Switzler
- *Predictably Irrational*, Dan Ariely, PhD
- *Mandala of Being*, Richard Moss, M.D.
- *Awake at Work*, Michael Carroll
- *The Mindful Leader: 10 Principles for Bringing out the Best in Others*, Michael Carroll
- *The Untethered Soul: the Journey beyond Yourself*, Michael Singer
- *The 15 Commitments of Conscious Leadership*, Jim Dethmer
- *The 21 Skills of Spiritual Intelligence*, Cindy Wigglesworth
- *The EQ Edge*, Stephen Stein, PhD
- *Mindfulness and Psychotherapy*, Ronald D Siegel
- *On Emotional Intelligence*, Daniel Goleman, PhD
- *Daring Greatly,* Brené Brown PhD, LMSW

WEBSITES:
- Behavioral Economics- www.danariely.com
- Habits- www.jamesclear.com
- Free Meditation Project UCLA- www.marc.ucla.edu/mindful-meditations
- Living On Purpose- www.dungbeetle.org

APPS:
- Meditation- *Stop, Breathe, And Think*
- Seinfeld's 'Don't Break the Chain!' Goal App

ABOUT THE AUTHORS

From Austin, Texas, **Dr. Keith Kesler** is a Board Certified Psychiatrist, Psychoanalyst, and Certified Leadership Coach with over 35 years of clinical experience. He spent 15 years as a Board Certified Emergency Physician. Not surprisingly, his approach effectively utilizes practical, structured, and scientifically supported methods from neuroscience, behavioral economics, performance psychology, and perennial philosophy to integrate our human challenges. He helps clients with self-awareness and improving their Emotional Intelligence. In his work, Dr. Kesler addresses productivity and conflict resolution to help improve work performance and quality of life. Lest you think it is all work and no play, he is an instrument rated pilot, photographer, husband, father, and can 'scoot a mean boot' as a Texas 2-Step country dancer

Sarah Brisiel is an Integrative Wellness Coach, Communication Coach, and HR Consultant. She has over 15 years of Management and HR experience. She uses time-tested, data driven methods, as well as a firm foundation in organizational psychology to teach communication and conflict management skills. Her experience enables her to teach clients how to better understand each other (and themselves) in order to become more effective and productive. She lives in Austin and is an avid reader of all fiction, live music aficionado, and pet lover.

Keith and Sarah can be found online at
www.clinician2coach.com.

95062692R00052

Made in the USA
Columbia, SC
06 May 2018